631ART.COM PRESENTS:

"THE GOOD FIGHT"

A COLORING BOOK FOR PROGRESSIVES

BY EDDIE ALFARO

FREE
FO
AL
I AM A
SNOWFLAKE
and together
we are an
AVALANCHE
ICE
POLICY
IS
BROKEN

"NFANt ripped from
Mother's Breast at immigration
detention center, mother
handcuffed FOR RESISTING.

You CAN't FIX STUPID BUT YOU CAN VOTE it out
YOUR VOTE IS YOUR VOICE
REGiSTeR
VOTE HERE

"ANTI-VAGRANCY"
LAWS ARE CRUEL, COSTLY
and counter produc -tive.
HELP
* CRIMINALIZING HOMELESSNESS DOES NOT WORK!

FASCISM · IS · NOT · FREEDOM
SILENCE · IS · BETRAYAL
STAND UP
FIGHT BACK

BAN ASSAULT WEAPONS, HIGH-CAPACITY magazines, and BUMP STOCKS.

#MeToo
WE·BELIEVE·YOU
YOU'RE·NOT·ALONE
YOU'RE·NOT·tO·BLAME

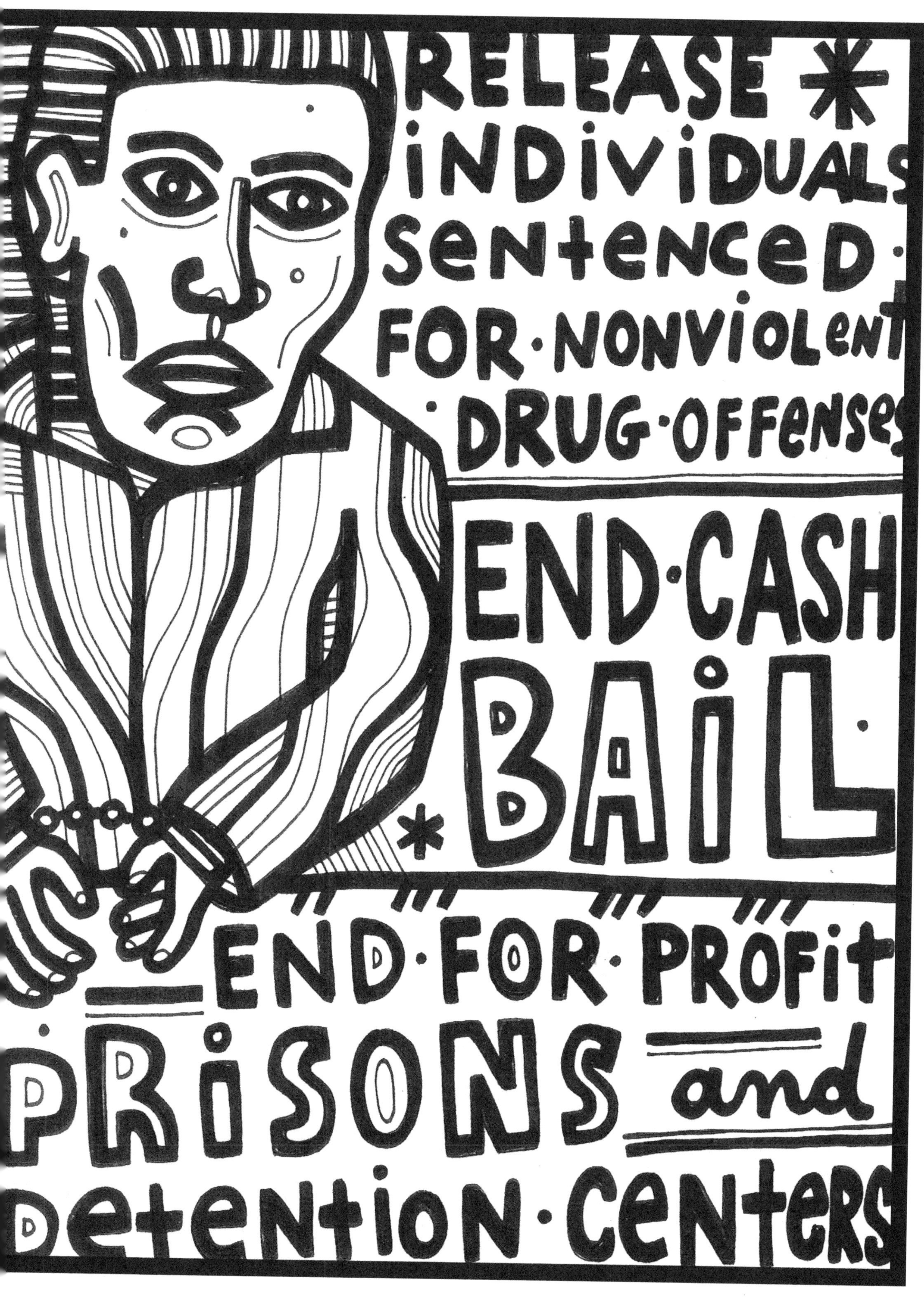

RELEASE * INDIVIDUALS SENTENCED FOR NONVIOLENT DRUG OFFENSES
END CASH BAIL
* END FOR PROFIT PRISONS and detention centers

I AM A SNOWFLAKE and together we are an AVALANCHE
I.C.E. POLICY IS BROKEN
FREE FO AL

MY
HEAR OUR VOICE
BODY
my
CHOICE
I STAND WITH PLANNED PARENTHOOD
FEMME & FIERCE

IMMIGRANTS MAKE·AMERICA GREAT
NO·KIDS IN·PRISON CAMPS!
CARE, DON'T U?
FREE·THE CHILDREN
KEEP·THE·KIDS DEPORT·THE·RACIST

Modern · SLAVES
ARe · Not · IN · CHAINS
they · are · in · DeBT
$55,212
t,361
$44,291

"There IS NO END IN SIGHt" Army major warns of "perpetual war" on terror
WAR ON PEACE
ETERNAL*WAR

the ONLY thing easier to BUY than a GUN IS A POLiticiaN.

There. ARE. more. than. 40,000 homeless Veterans IN. the. U.S.A.
Homeless vietnam. vet. PLEASE H.E.L.P.
NO. veteran. SHOULD. BE. without. A. PLACE. to. CALL. HOME.

BRAVE IS FIGHTING
AGAINST
INJUSTICE
BRAVE
IS MAKING
YOUR
VOICE
HEARD.
BRAVE
IS CARING
FOR OTHERS
BRAVE IS LOVE
IN THE FACE OF HATE.

THERE's POWER
IN PEOPLE
MAKE HUMAN
RIGHTS GREAT AGAIN!!!

THE POWER to HEAL
the POWER to CHANGE Lives
THE POWER to MAKE DREAMS COME TRUE. THE POWER TO unite
SUPPORT REFUGEE & MIGRANT children

LOCAL ACTION
NATIONAL
POLITICAL POWER!
CONGRESS HAS A 20% APPROVAL RATING, BUT HAS A 97% RE-ELECTION RATE
vote the BUMS OUT ON ELECTION DAY! YOUR VOICE YOUR VOTE
END THE CYCLE OF LEGALIZED CORRUPTION

Nearly EVERY iSSUe we FACe AS A NATiON iS caught iN the GRiP OF CORRUPTiON
MONeYeD iNTeResT'S get WHAT THeY WANT, AND THe ResT OF US PAY THe PRiCe

TELL CONGRESS
WE NEED NET
neutrality

STOP
MILITARIZED
ATTACKS
& CRIMINALIZATION
OF PEACEFUL
PROTESTERS

FIX OUR BROKEN POLITICAL SYSTEM
and RETURN TO A GOV. OF, BY, and FOR the PEOPLE
Every VOTER MATTERS!
VOTE
BALLOT BOX
EMPOWER the AMERICAN VOTER

UNItE
against
HATE
NEVER
AGAIN
NO to
NAZiS
MAKE
LOVE
NOt
WAR
LOVE
WINS

NO ONE IS
FREE WHEN
OTHERS ARE
oppressed

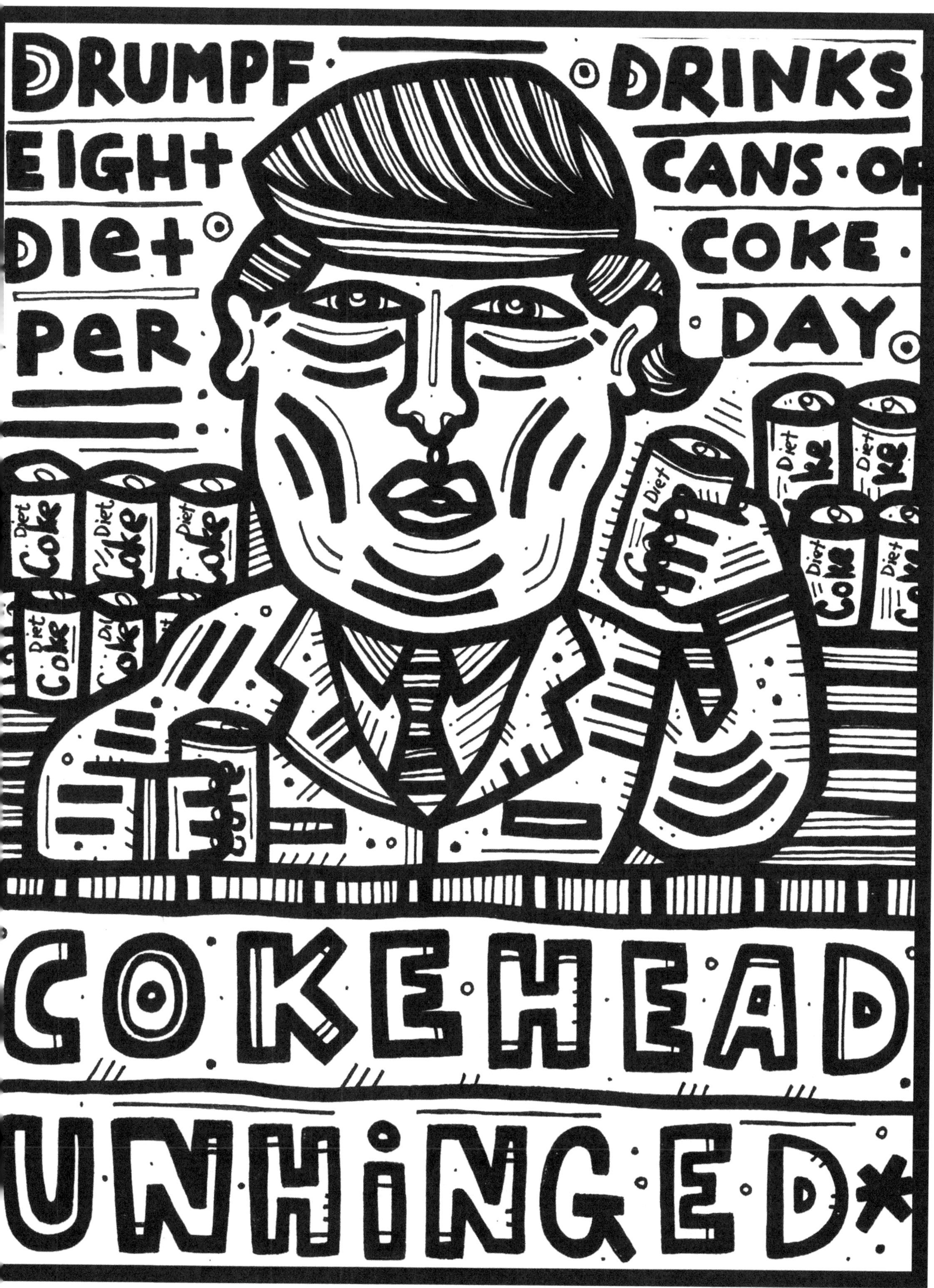

DRUMPF
EIGHt
DIEt
PER
DRINKS
CANS OF
COKE
DAY
Diet Coke
Diet Coke
Diet Coke
Diet Coke
Diet Coke
Diet Coke
Diet Coke
Diet Coke
COKEHEAD
UNHINGED*

TOTAL $$$
STUDENt LOAN
DEBt iN the US
is NOW AROUND
$1.3 tRiLLioN
STOP the FEDERAL GOV.
FROM MAKING A PROFIT ON STUDENt LOANS

UNITED
WE ARE
STRONG
MAKE THE CHANGE

WORKERS UPRISING
WE ARE WORTH more!
FAIR PAY
RESPECT
FOR WORKER RIGHTS!
WE ARE THE USA

TOGETHER
DUMP TRUMP
NOT MY PRES
TRUMP TYRANT! RACIST!
BIGOT
CAN'T BUILD A WALL HANDS TOO SMALL
UNITED WE R STRONG
STAND FIRM

All artwork in this book is free for you to use in your non-commercial use. Feel free to share it if you please.

artwork by:

Eddie Alfaro

eddiealfaro.com

sponsored by:

631art.com

the
end.